David Taylor, the well-known wildlife vet and regular guest on BBC television's *Animal Magic*, gives specialist, helpful and humorous advice on living with and caring for your cat. Everything the cat lover needs to know is presented with the aid of diagrams and some light-hearted cartoons.

THE CAT

An Owner's Maintenance Manual

DAVID TAYLOR, FRCVS

London
UNWIN PAPERBACKS
Boston   Sydney

First published in Unwin Paperbacks 1980

UNWIN® PAPERBACKS
40 Museum Street, London WC1A 1LU

British Library Cataloguing in Publication Data

Taylor, David, *b. 1934*
   The cat.
   1. Cats
   I. Title
   636.8′08′3   SF447 79-41534

ISBN 0-04-636011-5

Typeset in 10 on 11 point Times,
and printed in Great Britain
by Hunt Barnard Printing Ltd., Aylesbury, Bucks

Contents

A harmless, necessary cat
William Shakespeare: *The Merchant of Venice*, Act IV scene 1

Introduction

Do you suffer from ailurophilia? If so, you're in distinguished company. Pope Gregory I, Cardinal Wolsey, Richelieu, King Louis XV, Abraham Lincoln, Theodore Roosevelt, Sir Harold Wilson, Mussolini, Lenin, Doctor Johnson all had it in common. So does my charlady. So, in chronic, advanced form, do I. It is the love of mîw the sacred, of the Egyptian Goddess, Bast, of the inscrutable grimalkin, of *Felis catus L.*, the domestic cat.

There are a hundred good reasons for having a cat around. Economic to run, self-exercising, small and relatively silent, they are ideal for folk of limited means, for the old, for those who live in blocks of flats. Cats are easily acquired, unless of course your household mouser must be a Mexican Hairless or a Red Self Persian with a pedigree that reads like Doomsday Book. In the normal run of things, people just acquire cats or cats just acquire people. One walks in on the other and, if the stars are right for both the human and the feline side of the partnership, a permanent union develops.

I hesitate to use the word 'owned'. Cats, unlike dogs, do not take lightly to being 'owned'. Many cats own people. A cat's individuality, its 'self', is never up for grabs. So it is perhaps more accurate to say that a cat *sojourns* with its adopted homo sapiens.

Nevertheless, with such lodgers under one's roof, re-markably constructed athletes, not-so-distant relatives of the Lords of the Jungle, that have raised religions, toppled kings, drawn the thunders of the Vatican and the protection of princes, it is vital to look intelligently to their needs and

their foibles. Care for your guest well and he will reward you abundantly.

After all, look at the devotion lavished on that other family pet, the motor car, a comparatively crudely constructed, mindless beast, whose lineage and achievements can scarcely hold a candle to those of the cat. Sunday morning is the main time when owners of motor cars can be seen in driveways, back yards and by the kerbside up and down the country attending to the upkeep of their dumb brutes. Such humane concern for the metallic pet's well-being is admirable, extending as it does to treatment and prevention of minor complaints, cleaning of the anatomy and provision of a suitable, energy-producing diet. It is done with enthusiasm, various members of the family participating. The rules followed are those laid down in the vade-mecum that came with their pet, the Maintenance Manual.

By some oversight, cats do not normally come with their own Maintenance Manual, but what appears to be good for the relatively simple *Automobilus horrendus* must surely be even more so for *Felis catus L*.

Your love of cats I take for granted. What follows is concerned with practical matters, the running and maintenance of the Family Cat, and I see no reason for departing from the general approach used in the manuals prepared for Rolls-Royces or Cadillacs valued at a mere few thousand pounds.

1

Lat take a cat, and fostre him wel with milk,
And tendre flesh, and make his couche of silk.
Geoffrey Chaucer: *The Manciple's Tale*

This Year's Models

The domestic cat in Europe and America probably arose from a crossing of two wild species, *Felis sylvestris* and *Felis lybica*. The original tame cats were almost certainly tabby-marked and very similar to the true Wild cat that just survives in lonely Scottish forests. *Felis lybica*, the Kaffir cat, is larger and stockier than the modern moggy, with a light or orange-brown coat and narrow dark stripes. Found in forested regions of Africa and Asia, *Felis lybica* is even said to hang out still in parts of the holiday islands of Majorca, Corsica, Sardinia and Crete. A solitary, nocturnal hunter and wise with it, the cat keeps well clear of the suntan-oil brigade.

Other domestic breeds outside Europe similarly developed from small African or Asiatic wild cats. Abyssinian, Burmese and Korat cats still retain many of the physical characteristics of their feral ancestors, and the gap between them and such existing wild species as the Jungle cat of Egypt and Asia Minor, or the Manul of China, would seem to be narrow.

Thousands of years of cross-breeding led to the variety of breeds and colours available today. The chance creation of mutations over the ages produced hereditary oddities such as squint, stumpiness or absence of tails, polydactyly (a larger than usual number of claws) and duplicated ear-flaps. Some of these quirks are now the main features distinguishing certain breeds, for example hairlessness in the Mexican

Hairless cat and the lack of a tail in the Manx. The origin of that most superior of cats, the Siamese, is however wrapped in mystery. We know of no wild feline that might lay claim to being country cousin of a breed that is unique in appearance, voice and demeanour.

I will defend to the death the belief that all cats are equal. Each is a personality. Each brings delight, friendship, style. There are marginally better or worse mousers, there are more or less pronounced xenophobes, but by and large a cat is a cat is a cat with a full measure of the species' abundant virtues and rarely any vices. It is true, of course, that if all cats are equal, some are more equal than others, and the self-appointed exceptions to the rule must once again be the Siamese: no-one should go through life without having a Siamese at some stage to run the household.

The main breeds today are:

Longhairs (Persians)		*Shorthairs*	
Black	Shell Cameo	Abyssinian	Korat
Blue	Smoke	Black	Magpie
Blue Cream	Tabby	Blue	Manx
Calico	Tortoiseshell	Blue Cream	Red Spotted
Chinchilla	White	Blue Spotted	Rex
Colour Pointed		Burmese	Russian Blue
Cream		Chestnut Brown	Siamese
Himalayan		Domestic	Tabby
Red Self		Shorthair	Tortoiseshell
Shades Camel		Havana	White

There is also the ubiquitous, caterwauling, flower-bed-delving, sofa-shredding, hearth-adorning, dustbin-loitering, town and country Moggy.

All the above models are constructed and equipped to the same blueprint with an eye to producing one of the most perfectly adapted designs of small carnivore. The result of several aeons of prototype testing has been the evolution of an animal that is compact, efficient, independent and highly manoeuvrable. The combination of agility with muscular power, and the fitting of highly sensitive detection apparatus and a well-packed weapons system, make the cat an economic, mobile, all-weather hunter.

2

A German zoologist present at the 1960 Chilean earthquake reported that although house cats announced the arrival of tremors ten to sixty seconds before men could feel them (as did dogs, horses and pheasants), several captive pumas did not appear to notice a thing.

Specifications

WEIGHT

Average of adults, six to twelve pounds. Probably the heaviest domestic cat on record was a thirteen-year-old female tabby from the Lake District which topped forty pounds. The smallest of the wild cats, the Rusty-Spotted cat of India and Ceylon, rarely exceeds three pounds in weight.

BODYWORK

Cats are made of muscle elegantly sculpted in all the right places. Curiously, they stay in trim without having to spend any time working out in the gymnasium or jogging round the park. The stretching which all cats indulge in may somehow provide all the exercise necessary to keep the animals in fighting condition. A complete lack of conventional exercise and gross overfeeding by doting humans eventually produce obesity, but this generally does not bring with it the ill health and curtailed life which one would expect in dogs and their owners. I like Fat Cats.

The cat has a most elastic body. The backbone is held together by muscles rather than ligaments as in man, and this makes the spine very mobile. Shoulder-joint design permits the turning of the foreleg in almost any direction. In fact, the suspension of this model gives a near-perfect ride.

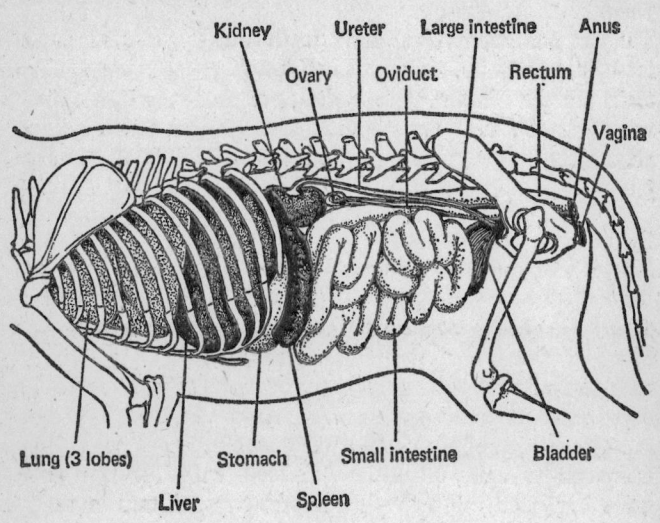

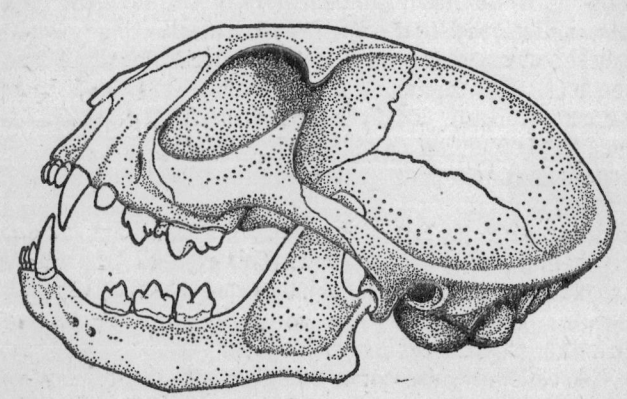

SPECIAL EQUIPMENT

Teeth

The cat has twenty-four milk teeth and thirty permanent teeth, sixteen in the upper jaw and fourteen in the lower. The teeth are the ultimate assassin's kit of the predatory carnivore and are designed to kill, slice and tear flesh. It is absolutely impossible for any grinding-type chewing to take place.

Eyes

Perfectly adapted to work well in the dimmest light. There is a light-intensifying screen of iridescent crystals set behind the retina which gathers every speck of available light and bounces it back onto the light-sensitive layers of rods and cones to give maximum receptivity. This crystal screen is what makes a cat's eyes flash fire in the dark. It is absent in humans who consequently waste much of what little light is around at night, unless they are soldiers using 'starlight-gathering', image-intensifying sniperscopes. Cats cannot see any better than humans in total darkness.

Cats do see in colour but not very well.

Hearing

The cat obviously has good hearing, and with thirty muscles working its ears, as compared with six in man, it can turn them precisely to locate sounds. This ear-turning is done far quicker than in the dog, although the dog, which can respond to frequencies of 35,000 cycles per second, hears ultra-sonic noise slightly better. The cat's range extends only to 25,000 cycles, the human's to 20,000.

Smell

Cats are great sniffers and respond particularly to odours containing nitrogen compounds. This explains why rancid or just slightly 'off' food, which releases chemicals rich in nitrogen, is immediately rejected by Puss, who flicks a paw irritably and stalks off in high dudgeon.

The cat's nose also comes complete with highly sensitive thermo-receptor nerve endings that can detect heat or cold.

Touch

The function of cats' whiskers is not fully understood. Something to do with touch, yes, and removing them can distinctly disturb a cat for some time.

There is no substance in the belief that a cat's whiskers protrude on each side to a distance equal to that of the animal's maximum width, so enabling it to gauge whether or not it can pass through a given space without touching anything and perhaps making a give-away noise when stalking prey. But in the dark, a cat's whiskers are immensely sensitive and rapid-acting antennae; simply, their owner uses them to identify things which he cannot see. Scientists have suggested that if a cat's whisker touches a mouse in the dark, the cat reacts with the speed and precision of a mousetrap. Other scientists speculate that the cat may bend some or all of its whiskers downwards when jumping or bounding over the ground at night. Certainly the little desert jerboa uses two of its whiskers to do this: the

downward pointing whiskers are used to detect stones, holes or other irregularities in the animal's path. Even when the jerboa is going at full speed, it can take avoiding action while in the air or on the ground by changing the direction of the body in a split second. Maybe cats use their whiskers in the same way.

Apart from touch, cats are highly sensitive to vibrations. Like some other species, they may give warning of a coming earthquake. There were widespread reports of strange behaviour by house cats in the ten to fifteen minutes preceding the disasters at Agadir, Skopje, Chile and Alaska in the 1960s. Village peasants on the slopes of Mount Etna keep cats as early warning devices. When the fireside tom ups and makes for the door hell-for-leather for no apparent reason, the human occupants follow hotfoot.

Claws

There is a convenient claw-sheathing mechanism activated by muscles that not only act like a flick-knife spring but also spread the toes for maximum effect. The same system is built into the larger models (tigers, lions, leopards etc) but is absent in that curious, dog-like cat, the cheetah.

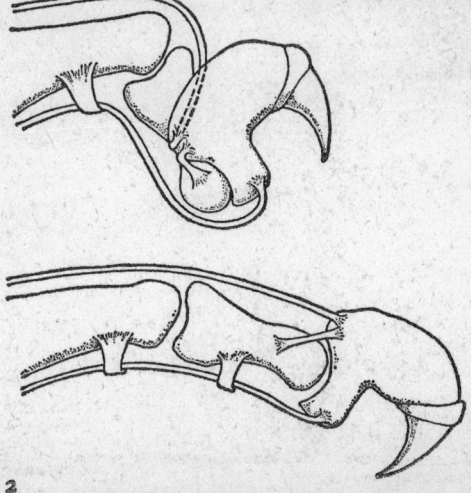

Homing Device

Purring is installed. This sound is not a 'voice' coming from the larynx but is the vibration of the blood in a large vein in the chest cavity. Where the vein passes through the diaphragm, the muscle sheet separating chest from abdomen, contraction of muscles round the vein 'nips' the blood flow and sets up oscillations, the sounds of which are magnified by the air-filled bronchial tubes and windpipe.

Purring can be heard, but more importantly can be felt as a vibration. Kittens, born blind, without sense of smell and with undeveloped ears, react strongly to the purring vibrations and make for Mum and the safety and suckling she affords. It is interesting to note that feline mothers stop purring as soon as the kittens begin to suckle; the homing device has done its stuff. We do not know why male cats purr.

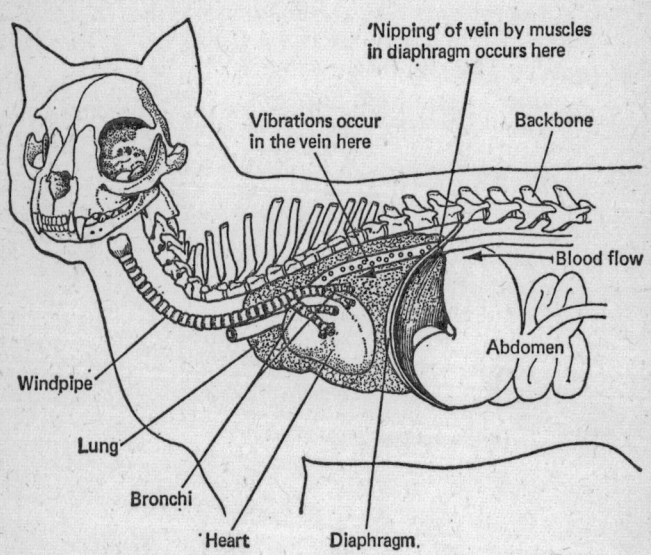

Incidentally, purring can sometimes be heard when cats are in extreme pain. What that signifies, no-one knows. Perhaps the chest blood vessel is 'nipped' by an involuntary nervous reflex.

Cooling System

'No sweat' would be a suitable motto for such cool characters as cats. They do not sweat like horses, perspire like men or glow like ladies. They lose heat by radiation from their body surfaces, which are much larger compared to their bulk than is the case with bigger creatures such as the dog or the horse. Occasionally they pant, but they do not indulge in the frenetic slobbering of common canines.

3

When Shakespeare's friend, the Earl of Southampton, was imprisoned in the Tower of London, his black and white cat broke into the fortress, sought out the right cell and entered it by shinning down the chimney; a contemporary painting showed the two of them doing 'porridge' together.

Performance

Intelligence

The yardstick most commonly used to measure intelligence in animals is to compare brain weight with the length of the great nerve called the spinal cord. This ratio, which represents how much grey matter is controlling how much body, has the advantage of being an objective assessment and should be bigger in more intelligent species.

A human gives a ratio of fifty to one, the marmoset monkey eighteen to one and the cat four to one. Make of that what you will!

Cats have generally been credited with sharp wits in stories throughout the ages from every nation. Sadly, however, Dick Whittington's famous cat in the pantomime story appears not to have been an animal of any sort; in fact his 'cat' was probably a cat boat, a one-masted vessel that carried coal and timber between the north-east and London and thereby made Whittington's fortune.

Locomotion

The cat can run at speeds of up to 27 mph, compared with 45 mph for a greyhound and 63 mph for a cheetah.

When walking, cats move the front and back legs on the same side simultaneously. The only other animals that do that are the camel and the giraffe – *very* distant relations!

Domesticated cats are indifferent swimmers. The Persian Swimming cat, a rare breed, is reckoned to be keen on taking a dip, but I once watched a few of them being dunked and encouraged to do the odd length in front of TV cameras. They were pictures of bedraggled unenthusiasm as pitiful as my own moggy when he falls into our pond while poaching goldfish. Among wild cats the tiger is a strong swimmer as, for professional reasons, is the Fishing cat (*Felis viverrina*). The star water-baby of felines, however, is undoubtedly the jaguar, who takes to the water with energy and aplomb. What stroke do cats use when they swim? The dog paddle.

Jumping

The elasticity of their bodies, coupled with an ultra-fast nerve link between their inner ears, brain and muscles, enables cats to turn into a 'feet-down' landing position while falling at speed, even over short distances. They have been known to survive falls from nineteen-storey buildings (approximately 200 feet).

One of the weaker muscle areas in the feline body is in the neck. Consequently, although the back and limbs can usually absorb the shock with ease when their owner is landing from great heights, there is a tendency for the head to keep on travelling downwards and for the point of the chin to rap hard against the ground. Fractures of the lower jaw are very common in these cases, particularly in the tenement blocks and high-rise flats of cities such as Glasgow, where Puss is wont to doze on the window-sill in the balmy air of a summer evening. Trouble looms when one of the family unknowingly closes the window, dislodging the dreaming cat from his precarious ledge and launching him without ceremony into space.

Instinct

Leave your car stuck in a snow drift or have it pinched by joy-riders and there isn't a cat in hell's chance (no doubt because deceased felines end up in the other place) of it making its own way home. Automobiles are scatter-brained lumps.

Cats, on the other hand, often track down their homes with great fortitude, and have frequently travelled long distances to rejoin patrons who find favour with them. The longest recorded journey by a cat in search of its human associates is 950 miles, from Boston to Chicago.

Most cats that are taken along when the family move house raise no objection and quickly set about staking out their territory and arm-wrestling any felines on adjoining properties. Some, however, attached to the old homestead with its familiar hideaways, birds' nests, loose dustbin lids, dopier-than-average rodents and promiscuous members of the opposite sex, will have none of it and light out for their native land before the estate agent has handed over the keys.

This ability to make for home does not work if the family move house, leaving their cat behind; it is not possible for Puss to track them down in their new desirable residence if he has never visited it. It only works if the family home stays

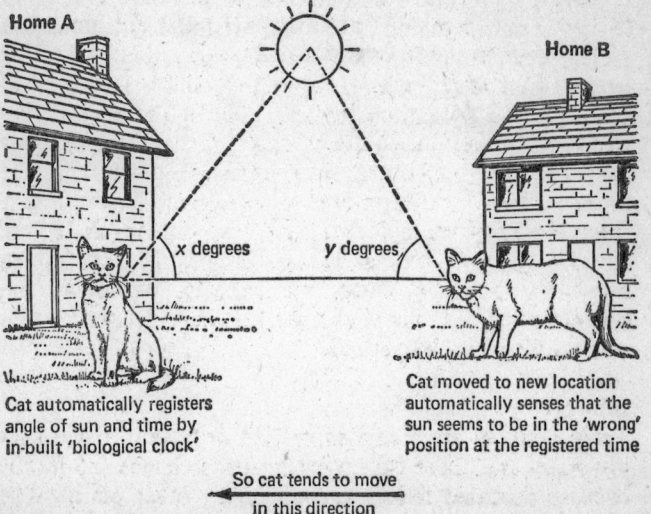

Home A

Home B

x degrees   *y* degrees

Cat automatically registers angle of sun and time by in-built 'biological clock'

Cat moved to new location automatically senses that the sun seems to be in the 'wrong' position at the registered time

So cat tends to move in this direction

put and the cat is hauled off to the back of beyond in a furniture lorry, cat-snatcher's van or similar vehicle. Freed, one hopes, at the end of the journey, the cat has a chance of plotting his route back to his own back yard.

Modern research suggest that the key to cat journeying of this sort lies in celestial navigation similar to that employed by birds. It works something like this:

During the months or years that the cat was living in the original home (A), his brain registered the angle of the sun at certain times of day. How does the cat tell what time it is without wearing a watch? Most animals, we believe, possess internal biological clocks. Certainly man and the higher mammals have them. They have been located in lowly creatures like cockroaches, too.

Now suppose the cat is uprooted to a new home (B), where the sun's angle at a certain time is slightly different. If he wants to put it right, the cat must begin by trial and error. In one direction he finds the angle gets worse. He tries another; the angle improves. That must be the direction to go. All this is a subconscious activity, of course, but gradually, in trying to get the sun into the right spot in the sky at the right time, Puss finds himself in a neighbourhood where the smells, sights and sounds are familiar. From then on it is plain sailing.

Next time you see your cat stretching on the garden wall, remember – maybe he is just checking that the house has not moved!

4

The Cat, if you but singe her Tabby Skin,
The Chimney keeps, and sits content within;
But once grown sleek, will from her Corner run,
Sport with her Tail and wanton in the Sun;
She licks her fair round Face, and frisks abroad
To show her Furr, and to be catterwaw'd.
     Alexander Pope: *The Wife of Bath her Prologue,*
                              from Chaucer

Acquiring a Cat

Unless you have set your heart on a particular pedigree for some good reason, the pleasures of having a cat can be fully enjoyed by adopting or being adopted by a stray. Humane society catteries are full of unwanted cats; grab the first healthy one you find and you will not be disappointed.

Apart from a visit to a breeder or a fortuitous crossing of paths, there are other ways of picking Puss. For example, the cat of your life might be in the stars. If you know the date of a particular animal's birth, there are astrologers willing to draw up its personal horoscope. By matching it up with your own, they say, you can increase the chances of a perfect relationship. For example Virgo cats (24 August–23 September) are predicted to be excellent, conscientious, dedicated, down-to-earth cats especially suited to Capricorn and Taurus owners.

Whatever reason you have for sharing your dwelling with a cat, remember that it is both a privilege and a responsibility. Cats are not dustbins who can survive on scraps, nor free labour who will keep the house clear of mice and their bellies full in the process, nor day-boarders who can be shown the door at nightfall. You may have paid a few pounds or nothing at all for it, but any cat is worth a great deal. In AD 936, Howel Dda, Prince of Wales, valued cats as follows:

Kitten 1 penny   Mouser 2 pennies

and a penny was a lot of bread in those days. Anyone killing a cat had by law to pay its worth in corn, holding it by the tail with its nose touching the ground and then completely covering it with a mound of grain.

The ancient Egyptians venerated the cat (which they called mîw) and lynched those who killed cats, even accidentally. No wonder they were defeated in 500 BC by Persian soldiers carrying cats tied to their shields; no Egyptian would risk injuring one of the sacred creatures.

PRE-DELIVERY INSPECTION

The difficulties about selecting one's cat are similar to those involved in buying a second-hand car. How to spot the faults? Is it really in good running order? Although it is unlikely to be an expensive mistake if you acquire a cross-bred cat with, metaphorically speaking, its gear-box full of sawdust or its mileage clock wound back, if you are buying pedigree stock you *must* get expert advice before parting with large sums of money for potential show champions. Undershot teeth, cross-eyes and curious toe formations might otherwise be passed off like rusty corners, slipping clutches and worn bearings.

For all cats, pedigree or not, the following list of points should be checked off by the prospective owner. Look for these. Just as if you were buying a gleaming new car, do not merely take the salesman's word. Walk round it, look at it, see that it has got four wheels on and that the paint is not scratched. If all is well, buy (if possible on approval) and then have the animal thoroughly overhauled as soon as possible by the vet. *Never* buy from back-street pet-shops or 'cat farms'. *Never* buy a kitten younger than ten weeks.

A cat should:

be alert and interested in its surroundings

move around readily with its head held straight

spring to the ground from table height with an easy, controlled movement

have clear, bright eyes without any white film (haw or 'third eyelid') showing

have clean ears, mouth and nose without discharges

have clean white teeth without accumulations of tartar, and salmon-pink gums and tongue

have a smooth, clean skin both to the eye and to the touch, with sleek fur composed of a full bushy undercoat and a glossy topcoat.

A cat should not:

suffer from diarrhoea

sneeze, cough or wheeze

appear to be in pain when touched or handled

show any trace of blood from anywhere

have any holes, breaks or blemishes in its coat

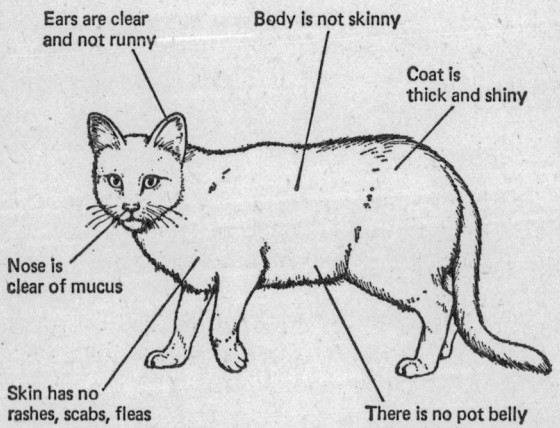

Ears are clear and not runny

Body is not skinny

Coat is thick and shiny

Nose is clear of mucus

Skin has no rashes, scabs, fleas

There is no pot belly

RUNNING IN A NEW MODEL

Diet

A kitten will have been weaned, beginning at four to five weeks, onto finely minced fish, meat, chicken and rabbit and should be well established on a 'grown-up' diet by eight weeks. Although essentially the same as for an adult cat (see pages 28–44), the menu should include two milk meals – I suggest breakfast and tea – in the day's total of four or five at this young age. Milk with cereals (any of the breakfast variety), porridge, groats or custard should be prepared and served warm at these meals. Tinned or bottled baby foods, yoghurt and invalid foods are also useful items that can be introduced into the diet. Give your kitten a catholic taste early and you will save yourself a lot of trouble later in his life.

Two health points: in countries with efficient water supplies for human beings, such as Britain and the USA, there is no need to boil water before giving it to your pet. Second, now that tuberculosis has been largely eradicated from dairy herds in these two countries, the once common intestinal TB so often seen in milk-drinking cats has virtually vanished. Nowadays I see more TB in zoo big cats than in their domesticated cousins; lions and tigers contract the lung form of the disease from keepers and spectators coughing in the vicinity of their cages.

Essential Servicing

Six weeks of age. Ask the vet to give the first shot of Feline Enteritis vaccine. (This is optional: you can wait till nine weeks but keep the kitten indoors away from other cats.)

Nine weeks of age. Time for the first shot of Feline Influenza vaccine. If the Feline Enteritis vaccine was not given at six weeks it can be combined with this now.

Twelve weeks of age. The second dose of Feline Enteritis and Feline Influenza vaccines are due.

Thirteen weeks of age. The kitten should now have a good active immunity against the serious feline virus diseases. Worm the kitten by administering one of the safe, highly efficient preparations (piperazine, mebendazole, dichlorvos, etc) available from your veterinarian. At the same time deal with any fleas in your kitten's coat by using a powder or aerosol. There are several kinds on the market. *Never* use DDT; consult your vet or pet-shop assistant.

Sixteen weeks of age. A good time to have a female kitten neutered ('spayed') if you do not intend to breed from her. This operation is done by a qualified vet under general anaesthetic. It consists of removing both ovaries and part of the horns of the womb. The incision is usually made in one flank. There is very little risk or strain involved in the operation; the kitten is bouncing around again twenty-four hours after the operation. Stitches are generally removed seven to ten days after the operation and there are rarely any after-effects.

Tom kittens can also be castrated at this age. Personally I recommend waiting until they are a couple of months older. This allows the penis to grow more in diameter and may avoid troublesome clogging-up with urine sludge later in life. Castration is the painless removal of the testicles by a vet. Although it can be done under local anaesthetic up to six months, after that age a full general anaesthetic is used. 'Doctored' toms do not necessarily become fat, sluggish and lazy. Nor are their mousing skills affected. Certainly their urine loses its pungent aroma and they become literally 'sweeter' characters.

Some folk think spaying and castration are cruel, a denial of a cat's natural desires. In practice, a castrated tom is spared the bites, abscesses and other unfortunate consequences of midnight battles on the rooftops. And there is a humane saving in unwanted pregnancies.

Both spaying and castration can be carried out if necessary at any age, though a vet will not usually want to spay a queen who is more than a couple of weeks pregnant. If possible it is best to avoid operating on a queen that is 'on heat': at these times the high level of sex hormones in her blood slows the speed of clotting when the vet operates.

In females, an alternative to the surgical approach is the Pill. These contraceptive tablets such as megestrol acetate can be used in one of two ways: half a five-milligram tablet daily for two months during the breeding season; or half a five-milligram tablet once weekly for up to one and a half years during the non-breeding season. Diabetic cats and certain others should not be put on the Pill, but before starting any regime you will discuss the best procedure with your vet.

Twenty weeks of age. Worm the kitten again. From now on repeat the worming every three months. Should worms of any kind be seen in the stools or stuck to the fur of the hind-end at any time, worm the cat at once. Modern worming drugs can be repeated without ill effect.

Annually. Make sure Puss is boosted against Feline Enteritis and Feline Influenza with a single injection by the veterinarian. Take the opportunity to let the vet give your cat a thorough overhaul. If tartar is beginning to build up on the teeth it can be painlessly removed by dental scrapers or ultra-sound machines at the surgery.

When you go on your summer holiday, your cat will be happier at home if you can make arrangements for a reliable neighbour to pop in and see to his needs each day. If possible, avoid sending him to a cattery. If you have to do so, keep a sharp eye on him when he comes back. If he shows any sign of ill health, seek professional advice. Bugs make hay while the sun shines, owners are on holiday and cats are making the best of their compulsory Summer Camp. Viruses and bacteria thrive in the warmth and humidity of often over-populated cat houses. Certainly de-flea your cat on his return.

SECOND-HAND MODELS

Taking over an older cat is not difficult. If he or she walks in on you, it is a piece of cake. If you inherit, purchase or are otherwise presented with a mature feline, the general rules laid out in Pre-Delivery Inspection (pages 20–2) apply. Certainly have the new arrival examined by a vet. Worm it and, unless you are sure that it has been vaccinated against the major virus diseases, have it protected with the initial two-shot course as in kittens, followed by annual boosters. If it should turn out that the cat had been vaccinated previously, re-vaccinating him will not do a scrap of harm.

If it is an old-timer, there is still no reason why neutering should not be done. Obviously in really ancient individuals passed down by, say, a deceased maiden aunt, we can afford to make an exception and forgo surgery so late in life.

Try to find out what the cat was fed on by his former owners. You may then find it easier to wean him out of his

HEH HEH

fads on to a broader diet by gradually sneaking new items into his favourite nosh.

Registration Plates

All cats should receive their registration plates as soon as you acquire them. Fit a leather collar *with an elasticated insert* to avoid the animal being strangled when tree-climbing. Attach to this a disc or tiny cylinder with the name, address and telephone number of the wearer's home. Add a bell, too, if you feel that it will foil his bird-napping forays. I am not so sure. Some of my cats which wore bells came home proudly bearing us gifts of dead sparrows and blue-tits so often that I could almost believe that they hunted on three paws with the fourth muffling the tell-tale clapper beneath their throats.

What Cat's averse to fish?
Thomas Gray: *On the Death of a
Favourite Cat, Drowned in a Tub of
Gold Fishes*

5

Fuel for your Cat

The correct collective name for a crowd of cats is a clowder; let us now consider rustling up chowder for the clowder!

There is much mumbo-jumbo preached by breeders,

kennel owners and cat fanciers on the subject of feline nutrition. Puss is not a pernickety machine, always liable to run badly or to 'pink' if his tank is not filled with precisely the right grade of fuel. Brought up correctly, he is not faddy. He insists more than most on high standards of freshness and hygiene in the kitchen, but otherwise is easily victualled in a wide variety of ways. Millions of words have been written by experts on the minutiae of acting as maître d' to one's cat. Let's cut the cackle and keep it simple.

True, cats are basically carnivores, but not exclusively so. Among wild cats, the Flat-headed cat (*Felis planiceps*) is the only species which feeds on vegetation to any extent – it has a particular love for fruit and sweet potatoes. But lions and tigers, after making a kill, will usually go straight for their victim's stomach, neglecting the prime fillets and

porterhouse to devour the soup of digesting vegetation. Even the Fishing cat (*Felis viverrina*) whose diet, lucky fellow, consists largely of molluscs, shrimp and fish, is known to have a penchant for seasoning his bouillabaisse with chewed mouthfuls of wild garlic and water weed.

Domestic cats should follow the lead of their wild cousins. Their diet should be varied and contain things other than meat and fish. Although you are unlikely to be going as far as Dr Johnson whose cat, Hodge, had the servants scurrying to and from Billingsgate with prodigious quantities of oysters to tickle the feline palate, many folk still overdo the raw meat content of their pet's diet.

Nothing but fish can lead to vitamin B_1 deficiency.

Nothing but liver can upset the bowels.

Nothing but prime lean meat produces calcium and vitamin deficiencies.

Variety is the key principle to be observed in feeding cats. Unless you inherit an old animal set in his ways (and even then there is a fair chance that a bit of culinary effort will winkle him out of an apparent determination to fast unto death unless given a monotonous diet of crayfish or caviare), accustom a kitten to a broad selection of foods.

This variety, as long as it supplies adequate quantities of all the essential nutriments, enables the cat to balance his diet for himself instinctively and automatically. It is easier and more economic for the owner. The use of fats and carbohydrates as energy sources makes good sense; an all-protein diet of meat or fish is wasteful in that some of the expensive foodstuff is simply burnt by the cat's body to provide calories, apart from the fact that it can be unhealthy in other ways.

Whatever you do, when acting as chef to a newly arrived Puss, introduce your diet gradually. Change him from the old menu to the new bit by bit over a couple of weeks or so.

Table 1 illustrates the general scientific principles worked out in laboratories as to the make-up of an ideal feeding regime.

Table 1. *General Feeding Principles*

Constituent	Recommended percentage of total diet (by weight)	Source
Protein	Adults: 25% (as compared to 13% in dogs) Kittens: 35–40%	Meat, fish, egg, cheese, milk
Fat	25–30% (much more than in the dog)	Animal and vegetable oils and fats
Carbohydrates	Up to 33% Not essential – cellulose is not digested but gives good 'bulk' action	Potatoes, cereals, bread
Vitamins: A		Milk, egg, liver, cod liver oil, carrots
B		Meat, liver, yeast, vegetables (some is synthesised by the cat in its own intestine)
C	See page 40. Beware of overdosing some vitamins	Fruit, vegetables, grass
D		Cod liver oil, milk, eggs, oily fish (herring, sprat, pilchard, etc)
E		Cereals (wheat germ) and some meat
Water	Provide *ad lib.* Most cats need around 30 cc per lb. body weight per day	
Minerals	A balanced diet in other respects provides enough balanced minerals (but see pages 52–3 about nursing mothers)	From all items of diet in various amounts

Food quantities

The boffins have calculated that the daily requirements of a cat on a diet containing 25 per cent protein is half an ounce of food per pound of body weight, but this is a theoretical guide only. In practice, like their human companions, cats vary widely in appetite. The ancient Greeks believed that cats put on weight as the moon waxed and lost weight as it waned. As we have seen, obesity does not generally lead to the health problems for cats that it does for dogs: show cats may need to have their outlines watched but the fireside moggy is a different case. Feed him up.

Frequency of feeding

Table 2 suggests how many meals a day a cat should have at each age of its life. Fresh food and water is a 'must' for cats. They have the nose of an Egon Ronay inspector and will stalk away from the first hint of staleness. Fresh food frequently avoids waste and the risk of tummy upsets.

Table 2   *Frequency of Feeding*

Age	Number of meals suggested per day
At weaning	6
4–5 months	4–5
6–7 months	3–4
7–8 months	3
over 9 months (adult)	2–3 (but see pages 52–3 for pregnant queens)
Senior citizens	See pages 61–4. May need 2–6

Puss can go without food for weeks and lose 40 per cent of his body weight without dying, though a 10–15 per cent loss of the total water in the cat body is normally fatal. Chips, a marmalade tom from Liverpool, was inadvertently packed into a wooden crate with some machine parts and survived a sea journey of four weeks to Mombasa. He was thought to have eaten some of the grease coating the machinery and to have lapped what little condensation moisture might have developed. Although he tottered out

like a skeleton when the crate was opened in Africa, he rapidly gained weight and condition in a local clinic and was flown back to England in VIP style two weeks later.

If Chips went through hell, what can one say about Thumper, a 2½-year-old tabby from Westminster who in 1964 was rescued from a lift shaft after being trapped for fifty-two days? Thumper's starvation diet had consisted of the occasional spider and cockroach and sips from a small puddle of oily water.

THE MAJOR FOODS

If we are agreed that variety is the spice of a cat's creature comforts, it is obviously impossible to lay down a fixed diet sheet. So many different foods are available to the thoughtful cat-minder that the suitable combinations are numberless. I shall therefore deal with the major kinds of food, mentioning any outstanding virtues or vices.

Protein

The protein foods form the central core of a carnivore diet.

1 The dried, soft-moist and canned foods (see pages 37–9).
2 Meat. This may be beef, lamb or pig. Raw meat is good occasionally and should be minced. Get it from the butcher's, not from the knacker's yard where it is likely to be cheap but teeming with Salmonella or even worse bacteria. Cooked meats should be baked or grilled rather than boiled to retain nutriments and tasty juices. If meat is boiled, however, the water should be seasoned and used as a gravy on some drier item of food. Offal (lungs, tripe, udder etc) should always be cooked. All cooked meat should be cut into small cubes before feeding.
3 Poultry. Scraps of cooked birds left over from the family table provide good pickings for Puss. Few humans pick a chicken carcass clean of such parts as the kidneys or parson's nose and they are greatly prized by cats. Most bird bones are splintery and should not be fed.
4 Rabbit. As for poultry.
5 Egg. A good source of protein, but better fed cooked and chopped rather than raw. Raw egg white contains a chemical called avidin which neutralises biotin, an essential vitamin, making it unavailable to the cat. A total of two eggs per week is the maximum for a cat. Separated egg yolks can be given more often if you wish – cats and meringue mixtures go together!
6 Milk. Not all cats like milk. If yours does not, why worry? It can hardly be regarded as a natural food for an adult carnivore. Water is always necessary for cats; milk is not. Some cats cannot digest the milk sugar (lactose) contained in cows' milk and get diarrhoea after drinking it.
7 Cheese. Excellent either raw (if grated) or cooked with some other item.
8 Fish. Fresh raw fish, chopped and boned if from a species larger than a herring, is admirable up to once or twice a week. Cooked fish is better steamed or baked

rather than boiled, again to retain maximum nutriments. Tinned fish such as sardines or pilchards can be given whether in oil or tomato sauce; the oil has a beneficial effect on the bowels and helps to dispel stomach 'fur-balls' that accumulate particularly in long-haired cats. Diets composed of nothing but fish are unbalanced and eventually produce problems, although it is not true to say as some books do that excess fish 'releases poisons' or causes the skin disease wrongly named 'Fish Eczema'.

Fillers

The filler foods are the sources of energy, bulk and fibre.

1 Vegetables. Boiled potato can be added to meat or fish up to around one-third of a meal. Start a cat early on such things as cooked cabbage, boiled young nettles, scraped raw carrot.

2 Starchy foods. Crumbled toasted bread can be used like potato and mixed with gravy or fish stock. Likewise pasta such as macaroni, spaghetti or noodles. Corn flakes, wheat flakes, porridge or baby cereal can all be used with milk, particularly for the first meal of the day and in kittens.

3 Fruit. If your cat fancies the occasional segment of tangerine or slice of apple (and it is surprising how many do), good for it! It is thought, incidentally, that 75 per cent of all cats are partial to the odd sweet grape.

Water

As long as fresh clean water is always available, worry not about how much of the stuff your feline lodger is drinking, unless you have settled for the lazy man's diet of nothing but dried food pellets (see page 38). Some cats do not appear to drink anything, at least not within sight of their owners. Of course they may be tippling at some favourite outdoor puddle or, like mine, inexplicably drawn to bath water (containing bath oil) or lavatory pans (containing blue deodorant). If your cat really does seem to do without

H_2O, there is no cause for concern; it is a common phenomenon. For one thing, on diets containing such things as cooked fish, tripe and certain tinned foods, the water in the food itself is a significant quantity to a creature the size of a cat. For another, small creatures get a large proportion of their daily water requirements by chemical action – the fats and carbohydrates in their food are 'burnt' within their bodies and produce water molecules. Bigger animals have the same water-producing mechanism but also need much more water so this source is of little significance to them.

We should perhaps pause at this point to doff our hats in memory of one, Jack, a black tom living in Brooklyn, who in 1937 at the age of three gave up water-drinking for milk laced with Pernod. As he grew older he demanded stiffer and stiffer saucers of 'milk' until it was a question of lacing the Pernod lightly with milk. Jack gave up the ghost in the bar where he lived when he was eight years old. At the post mortem his liver was found to be in a sad state. Jack just might have been interested to know that cats given steady

alcoholic diets appear to be more resistant to atomic radiation than their teetotal brethren, although I have no idea what conclusion to draw from this piece of useless scientific information.

So then, in feeding your cat ring the changes frequently with all the foods I have mentioned, but avoid Pernod and other hard liquor unless you are particularly anxious to own a radiation-proof moggy. A useful guide is to give *two parts by weight of a selection from the protein foods to one part of fillers.*

PRE-PACKED FOODS

There are three main kinds of pre-packed foods on sale for cats nowadays. Although all of these proprietary types claim to be complete diets, they almost certainly do not provide the nutritional completeness that a cat demands if he is to live long and strong. They are also monotonous as the sole item of diet and they are frequently very expensive in terms of what you are paying for their nutritive value.

All three types of pre-packed cat food, valuable and convenient though they may be, should therefore be used only as part of the full diet.

Canned food

These products consist of meat and/or fish, salts, jellying agents, vitamins, colouring chemicals, water and sometimes cereals. Advantages: in most cases very nutritious, they can form a large proportion of a cat's ration, store well and are sterile. Disadvantages: relatively expensive – you are buying a fair quantity of water, particularly where the 'jelly' is much in evidence – and the canning process and storage time may result in a drastic reduction of the vitamin level, particularly heat-unstable vitamins such as vitamin B.

Soft-moist products

They look good, taste not quite as good and contain meat, soya bean, fats, vitamins, preservatives, colouring chemicals and often thickening agents and sugar. Advantages: again

they are usually very nutritious and, if accepted, can make up a large proportion of the diet; you are buying less hidden water and they store reasonably well. Disadvantages: they are expensive, do not store as well as canned or dry foods and are generally too low in fat.

Dry food

These mini-biscuits come in all shapes and flavours and almost all cats will scoff one variety or another. They contain cereals, fish, meat, yeast, vitamins, fat and the ubiquitous colouring agents. Advantages: many kinds are fairly well balanced, they are cheaper and contain less water than canned or soft-moist food, store well and are pleasant to handle. Disadvantages: they are frequently much too low in fat content for cats and if fed exclusively have been suspected of causing bladder problems and difficulty in passing urine. Their low water content, together with the salt analysis of some brands, may tend to produce 'sludge' in the cat's urine which can block up the animal's waterworks. Where much dry food is fed, adequate fresh water must be available at all times and best of all the pellets may be moistened by gravy, milk or water. Use dry foods sparingly if at all for cats with a history of urinary troubles. Probably the best rule is to use them for all cats but, as I keep saying, as only one item in a varied menu.

Of course the last word on these multi-million pound products of the pet-food industry's cohorts of nutritionists, researchers and public relations executives lies with the ultimate consumer – Puss. Little does it influence him what mouth-watering plugs for such goodies flash on the TV screen whilst he drowses contentedly on top of the set. No ad-man ever yet persuaded a single cross-eyed tom to change his mind. A cat either likes it or not. Why, is none of your business. It is a personal, subjective, private matter. Cats keep their counsel.

SUPPLEMENTS AND SEASONING

With a broad diet as outlined, special vitamin and mineral supplements should not normally be needed.

Most cats, if brought up as discerning trenchermen, prefer intelligent seasoning of their food. I have had cats who adored curried chicken and spaghetti with garlic and clam sauce – very civilised and utterly beneficial. If cooking some of your pet's meals, season with iodised salt to taste (your taste). Enough iodine, which is a trace element, can be assured in this way. It is particularly important in pregnant queens, where iodine is needed to prevent resorption of the foetuses within the womb. Valuable gravy containing all essential salts can be made from Marmite or bouillon cubes. If you are using much proprietary dry or soft-moist food, remember that these products tend to be low in fat content, so add eight teaspoonsful of vegetable oil (sunflower, corn or olive) per pound of the proprietary food.

Having laboured like Mrs Beeton over your moggy, do not be alarmed if he still insists on chewing grass and weeds at the first opportunity. Grass is good for cats. It contains certain vitamins and also acts as an efficient emetic, helping the animal regurgitate unwanted matter such as fur-balls. If you and your cat share a flat without ready access to a garden, grow him some from seed in a window-box. Chewing grass is *not* a sign that the cat feels ill.

A CAT MAY LOOK ON A KING

Before going further, what about this repast for a Royal cat? Tsar Nicholas I of Russia instructed his Chef de Cuisine at St Petersburg in 1829 that his cat, Vashka, born on the day that the Russians prevailed in the Russo-Turkish War, should henceforth have prepared and served on an enamelled dish each day what he, the Tsar, considered to be the favourite food of the noble animal:

2 watchglasses-full of best Beluga black caviar
2 watchglasses-full of golden caviar

The above to be poached lightly for three minutes in rich Champagne. Then add the finely minced meat of one Edible Dormouse imported from France and turned until gold in unsalted hot butter, the yolk only of one woodcock's egg and a spoonful of fresh hare's blood. Broil in thick cream the whole. Sprinkle the cooled mixture with chopped chervil and the dried cheese of Sukhumi. Moisten (on hot days) with brut Champagne.

The sixteenth-century proverb says that 'A cat may look on a king' – no wonder with meals like that! I trust Vashka lived to a ripe old age on his epicurean fare, for it is not recorded. Despite the extravagance of the Tsarist recipe, it is remarkably balanced by modern scientific standards. And Tsar Nicholas and I agree on one thing at least – the need for variety in catering for cats.

THE FALLACIES ABOUT MOUSING...

Cats hunt mice, birds, insects and so on for sport, not as a food source. True, they may on occasion eat part or all of their prey, but basically they are in it for the fun of the game rather like humans in pink coats who rarely tuck into fox pie after making a kill. So you need not think that by underfeeding, or indeed not feeding your cat, he will be encouraged to clear your premises of small rodents. Quite the opposite. Well-fed cats are better mousers. They have the stamina, energy and quick reactions required for the sport. Castrated toms make just as good mousers as uncastrated ones.

Mickey, a well-fed tabby of Burscough in Lancashire, killed over 22,000 mice in 23 years before dying in 1968, an average of nearly three mice per day throughout his life.

... AND ABOUT FLIES

'Cats that catch flies and eat them go thin' is a very common saying. Although there is a possibility that a cat eating a bluebottle might also take in disease bacteria, the problem is a minute one. Occasionally worm eggs might be carried by flies from one cat to another. But do not fret about it: fly-eating cats rarely come to any harm and can be as plump as Christmas puddings.

THE GRIM OTHER SIDE OF THE COIN

Humans have sometimes eaten cats, and not just under wartime or siege conditions. The Trobriand Islanders used to roast a galantine of cat stuffed with fat mice on ceremonial occasions. Closer to home, the French seem to have produced the largest number of bizarre cat eaters. The famous glutton of the early nineteenth century, Tarrare of Versailles, liked to eat a whole raw cat, regurgitating a ball

of skin and fur half an hour after his meal like a bird of prey. This fellow also adored meals of raw snake, but a contemporary of his, a porter at the Jardin des Plantes in Paris, outdid him in possessing an even more depraved appetite: for big cats! The *Dictionnaire des Sciences Medicales* reports him consuming the body of a lion that died of disease in the menagerie. Although the lion seemed to agree with him, he was to expire eventually from violent colic following a simpler meal of eight pounds of hot bread.

Cat stealers still pass off dressed cat carcasses as rabbit for sale to the public. Where skin, head and feet have been removed it is not all that easy for the layman to tell the difference.

6

Mrs Crupp had indignantly assured him that there wasn't room to swing a cat there; but, as Mr Dick justly observed to me, sitting down on the foot of the bed, nursing his leg, 'You know, Trotwood, I don't want to swing a cat. I never do swing a cat. Therefore what does that signify to me!'

Charles Dickens: *David Copperfield*

Garaging your Cat

Cats, like cars, tend to get stolen, scratched and weatherworn if parked outside night after night. Responsible owners provide adequate cover at all times for their pride

and joy. Certainly many cats enjoy rambling in the open air, but the practice of 'putting the cat out' before going to bed can only lead to disease, injury and perhaps unwanted pregnancies. The easiest compromise for man and cat is to install a cat flap in one of the outside doors of the house. Otherwise make sure that Puss is home before lights out.

Cats can live virtually a total indoor life without suffering in health or happiness, since they can exercise themselves adequately in a very small space, but there are two important aspects of the Indoor Cat to prepare for: sanitation and scratching.

Sanitation

Cats are clean creatures and train quickly to relieve themselves outdoors or in a sanitary tray. Very old cats may become forgetful or lose control on occasion. Bear with them – you may be venerable yourself one day. Kittens soon get the idea if they are put in the garden or on the tray after waking and after meals.

A sanitary tray should be made of metal or plastic and be large enough for the cat actually to stand in. It should be lined with newspaper and then covered with a 1½ inch-deep layer of peat moss or one of the proprietary cat litters available at the pet-shop. Ashes can be used, though they are rather dusty. Sawdust is messy when dry, and quickly becomes soggy and smelly when wet. Remove the soiled litter daily and clean and disinfect the tray weekly, using any household disinfectant except those containing phenol, carbolic acid or any coal tar chemicals; these can poison cats by absorption through the skin. Rinse a disinfected pan thoroughly: Puss may refuse to use a lavatory reeking of antiseptic.

Scratching

This is in more ways than one a very touchy subject, particularly if Puss has no eye for interior decoration and takes it out on your Louis Quinze escritoire or the sofa that was your mother-in-law's wedding present. Why do cats scratch? There are several theories – as a way of sharpening the claws, as a form of stretching, as a visible territorial marking system. Personally I prefer the idea that it is simple manicuring – removing the husks of outer shell that form so rapidly on the feline claw.

The answer is to provide a substitute scratching object of the right texture to give the cat the most satisfying 'feel'.

A log complete with bark, a vertical post on a stand wrapped in coarse sacking or one of the compressed blocks of corrugated paper sold in pet-shops will do. Cats have to be trained to use these devices. At the first sign of Puss contemplating the furniture, grab him and take him to the official scratching point. With a little patience, he will get the message. Surgical removal of a cat's claws under anaesthetic by a vet is possible, but such mutilation for furniture's sake is indefensible.

Territorial marking

All cats, from lordly tiger downwards, are highly territorial animals. Your pet stakes out his patch of planet Earth as meticulously as any snow leopard. The 'boundary markers' that indicate the perimeter of his domain are patches of scent where he has sprayed urine. The smell of this urine is pungent and unpleasant to human nostrils and is most pronounced in uncastrated toms. Castration sweetens him up a treat. Be understanding if your cat seems to spit in your eye by puffing his odorous aerosol on your own door-step, window-ledge or even, but less frequently, on your shoes: he is just telling the feline world that you are his. Feel loved and reach for the Air-Wick with a smile.

Territorial marking is actually more complicated than it seems. The system allows two or more cats to operate in the same territory but without ever coming into conflict with one another. A cat out on the prowl can tell at a sniff whether a scent-mark is new or a few hours old. If it is new, the opposition may still be around and he changes his route. If it is old, he continues blithely on his way. Researchers studying domestic cats living free on bomb-sites and similar places have found that several individuals can patrol the same piece of territory without ever coming face to face by using it according to a definite timetable, rather like shared ownership of a holiday flatlet.

Sleeping arrangements

A special bed in a box or basket can be provided if you wish, but it is not essential. Most cats pick their sleeping places around the house quite independently. Young kittens should, however, be given a box (a simple cardboard one will do) in which they can sleep snug, draught-free and out of harm's way. A lining of newspaper covered by a piece of blanket which is changed regularly must be placed inside. To avoid contamination by scraps of food, never feed a kitten in its sleeping box.

Why don't I believe in having my cats sleeping with me? Cats, like any animals which live close to the ground, sniff each other's backsides, investigate drains and can be too intimate with germ-carrying rodents, are more likely to transmit infections to humans if draped across the pillow eight hours out of every twenty-four. There may be a risk of suffocation of a very small baby if a cat is allowed into the room in which the infant is sleeping.

Having a cat around the house was once a truly perilous business. In 1484 Pope Innocent VIII denounced the cat and all who harboured it. At the time he was troubled by the flourishing in the Rhineland of a Teutonic cult centred upon Freya, a goddess whose chariot was said to be drawn by two black cats. As a consequence of the Papal wrath, cats and their owners were executed by the thousand.

7

The Assembly-line: Breeding Cats

I shall not deal with the minutiae of breeding pedigree animals for show purposes, the selection of handsome toms and the ceremonies attendant upon their honeymoons with beauteous queens. The fierce jealousies of the Cat Fancy are outside our compass, so I intend simply to plot a course through the miraculous process of bringing into the world a litter of healthy kittens, blue-blooded or proletarian.

If you do not want your cat to have or to father unwanted kittens, or if you cannot be certain of finding good homes for any kittens born, make sure your queen is neutered (speyed) or your tom castrated (doctored) or talk to your vet about the Pill. Otherwise, here we go.

Queens become sexually mature between seven to twelve months of age. Do not breed a queen until she is at least one year old, at which age cats breed most easily.

Queens come into heat (oestrus) according to a seasonal rhythm. They come into heat for two to four days at approximately two-week intervals. This cycle is repeated two or three times in spring (mainly March and April) and again in summer (mainly June and July) with sometimes a third period of activity in September. Not being dumb machines, some queens do their own thing and have heat cycles somewhat outside these main peaks.

You will know when a queen is in heat. She will call her beaux with a low, plaintive love-song or, in the case of Siamese, a powerful aria worthy of Callas. She will roll and wriggle more than usual, try to get out of the house and generally appear restless and fidgety. Most noticeable of all is the characteristic mating posture she will adopt: front end flat on the ground, rear end stuck in the air and hind legs 'pedalling' an invisible bicycle.

The cat is interesting in that eggs are popped out of the ovary (ovulation) only when mating actually takes place. Eggs are not wasted, as in humans and many other animals. When mating occurs, the act of coitus and particularly the firm biting of the back of the queen's neck by the tom send nerve impulses to a part of the brain. The information is passed on to the pituitary gland, which releases a hormone. The latter speeds quickly through the blood to the ovary and bursts a handful of ripe follicles. Out fall some eggs ready for fertilisation. The kittens are on their way.

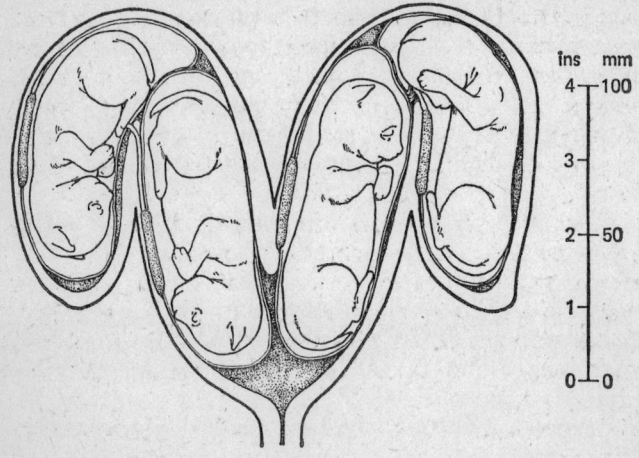

Pregnancy in the cat lasts 58 to 71 days with an average of 65 days. The number of kittens in a litter is three to five; the average litter size in the USA has been calculated to be 3·88 kittens. Actually, more than five eggs are usually fertilised in the queen's uterus. Probably twelve or more kitten embryos start developing but over half die back in the womb and are resorbed back into the bloodstream in the natural order of things.

Siamese tend to have larger and Abyssinians smaller litters. The biggest litter of kittens ever recorded is of thirteen to a one-year-old Siamese in Australia. A claim of nineteen (with four incompletely formed) has been made for a Burmese queen in England.

Pregnant queens need no special attention beyond plenty of good nourishing food. Healthy reproduction depends particularly on adequate protein, vitamin A, calcium and iodine. Our diet system (pages 28–44) copes with all that. Provide a pregnant mum with three or four meals each day.

As kittening approaches, the queen will look for a quiet place in which to deliver her babies. She is not likely to have any trouble and will want to be left alone. Dark corners are a favourite. If she has a special box, basket or blanket put it there. Providing the queen appears well, is eating, has not been seen straining (even just once) and has no discharges of any colour from her vagina, there is no need to panic if pregnancy extends beyond the average of 65 days.

When straining begins, a kitten should be born within *half an hour*. If none has appeared after *an hour and a half*, ask for veterinary advice. If no straining is seen but the queen appears unwell or has any amount of coloured (red, brown, yellow) discharge from the vagina without a kitten being born within *an hour and a half*, similarly ask for veterinary advice.

A queen should be provided with food and water during labour; many will eat or drink in the intervals between kittens arriving.

Most kittenings are normal and trouble-free. The kittens are born in a membrane sac rather like a deep-frozen chicken. On emerging into the world they either split out of this sac or are freed by their mother. Should you be present at the birth, watch to see that the kittens do get at least their head free from the sac to avoid suffocating. If there is any delay in the sac rupture, particularly where queens are having their first litter, wash your hands thoroughly and then peel out the kitten. If the umbilical cord is still intact and the mother has not chewed through it, break it by pulling it apart between the fingers of both hands about halfway between the placenta and the kitten. Never pull the umbilical cord away from the kitten's tummy; this could lead to a rupture or umbilical hernia. Queens may try to eat their placentas, which is a natural 'cleaning-up' instinct, but if possible dispose of any placentas lying around. During birth and the expulsion of the placentas (one for each kitten), you may notice a chocolate-brown discharge. This is normal.

After birth has been completed, leave Mum and her brood

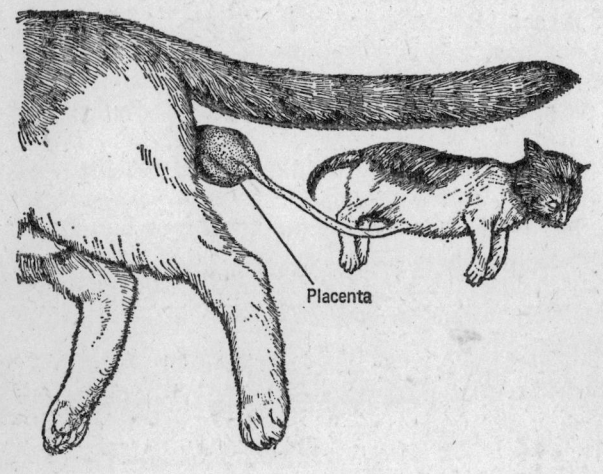

Placenta

in peace for a couple of hours and then move them to a clean new bed or at least renew the bedding where they are lying. There is no harm in handling the kittens occasionally each day.

Nursing mothers need extra food, particularly as the kittens grow bigger. Weaning usually begins at four to five weeks and the average length of lactation (milk production) is seven weeks. From four weeks onwards, actively encourage the kittens to supplement their diet with items other than mother's milk.

Newborn kittens begin suckling soon after Mum has licked them clean and never lose weight unless illness intervenes or the milk supply becomes inadequate. If in doubt, weigh the kittens daily.

Table 3   *Average Weight of Kittens*

Age (days)	Typical weight range (grams)
1	70–135
5	90–220
10	130–280
15	175–335
20	210–415
25	230–480
30	260–520
35	290–620
40	305–670
45	380–765
50	390–880

If a queen turns out to be a neglectful mother or is deficient in milk you have two choices – fostering or bottle-rearing – unless you decide to have unwanted kittens euthanased. In that case *never* drown kittens – it is obscenely cruel. Take them to the vet.

Fostering

If a foster mother is available, kittens can be transferred very successfully. Smear the kittens to be fostered with a little butter. Once the foster mum has licked the butter off, she will regard the foundlings as her own. Weighing is more important during fostering to check that the kittens really are getting enough milk.

Bottle-rearing

Although it is not difficult to bring kittens up on modified cows' milk, goat milk or Carnation milk, the easiest way is to buy one of the special proprietary cat milk substitutes such as Cimicat. Follow the instructions on the box and you should have excellent results. I have found that this works just as well for big cat cubs such as lion, tiger, leopard and puma. With cheetah cubs my best success has been with good old Carnation milk made up with lime water.

When a queen has to have kittens taken away from her for some reason, or if they die, do not worry about what will happen to her milk. Do not try milking it off – that will just stimulate more to be formed. Leave her alone and it will 'go back' quite naturally. Drugs to suppress the milk are rarely necessary and there is very little likelihood of mastitis (breast inflammation) developing.

At the end of lactation a lusty bundle of fast-growing kittens may continue to suckle the mother even though they are weaned. They can be taken away from Mum at ten weeks, but if you are keeping them on, please do not let them continue pestering the queen when her milk is drying up. She has done her bit and frequently looks thinner and in need of a good rest. Build her up with several more weeks of extra feeding and dissuade the young 'uns from raiding the milk bar by smearing her teats with a bitter mixture of vaseline and quinine or spraying her there occasionally with non-toxic repellant Curb aerosol.

Please, unless you really want to breed from your queen and can find homes for all her progeny, and if your tom is not a Robert Redford among the pedigrees, with breeders queueing up to lay down pounds and pounds for his amatory services, have them sterilised. There are more than a few individuals living a miserable life below the breadline among Great Britain's six million cats and the United States' twenty-eight million.

Finally, if you have a pedigree queen who accidentally has a mongrel litter by an alley tom, do not be misled by the old but still common belief that she is in some way spoiled for life and prevented from ever bearing perfect kittens when later mated legitimately. It just ain't so.

In the mid-nineteenth century a 'cat-skin' was the name for a cheap make of silk hat or the academic hood of a university graduate. Later the term, 'to get one's cat-skin' meant to obtain the BA degree.

Care of the Upholstery

Cats are either short-haired or long-haired. The former require little grooming by their owners, keeping themselves neat and tidy by washing themselves at every opportunity. Nevertheless it is a wise practice to inspect them every week or so, parting the coat to look at the condition of the skin, and grooming if there are any loose hairs about.

Long-haired cats need much more attention. Regular grooming with a soft brush and coarse steel comb every one or two days is essential. This prevents the two major effects of upholstery neglect: cots and stomach fur-balls.

Cots

Long hair left to its own devices easily tangles into tight balls which build up progressively into cots that can reach the size of tennis balls in some advanced cases. Any tangling of hair should be teased out at the earliest opportunity. When tight cots have formed, *never* try cutting them off with scissors: it is only too easy to lift the skin in the process and take a chunk out of Puss proper. Cases so far advanced need a vet to sedate the animal before breaking up and combing out the cots.

Fur-balls

While they groom themselves cats tend to take loose hairs into their mouths. Because of the backward-pointing rough scales on the surface of cats' tongues and the fact that they cannot spit, any hairs taken into a cat's mouth finally end up in the stomach. Here they build up into sticky, dark accumulations called fur-balls which look like dead mice when regurgitated. Regular grooming, the feeding of tinned fish in oil and the occasional dose of paraffin oil stop fur-balls becoming a problem.

Fleas

When inspecting the coat of any cat, look out for little visitors such as fleas or, less frequently, lice, ticks or keds. Fleas tend to scuttle nimbly out of the way of intruding human fingers but can easily be detected by the droppings they leave behind. If you see what looks like fine coal-dust in the coat, particularly around the neck and along the back, Puss has not been down the mines. The dust is the digested blood sucked by fleas and passed out in their stools.

Never use DDT to combat fleas. It is poisonous to cats. Get a modern anti-parasitic powder or aerosol from the vet or pet-shop. Collars impregnated with flea-killer chemicals do not work very well.

Cleaning

It is rarely necessary to bath a cat – only if it becomes heavily contaminated with something like oil or fertiliser. Oil and tar products should be removed as quickly as possible. They can poison a cat either by being licked off or by being absorbed directly through the skin. *Never* use paraffin or petrol to remove contaminating substances from cat fur. Cotton wool dampened in alcohol (methylated spirits) is permissible for small spots. Heavily contaminated animals really do need veterinary attention.

Bath your cat if you must in warm water (about five inches deep) and use good quality baby soap or baby bubble bath. Never use carbolic or coal tar soap. Rinse thoroughly and dry with soft towels and a hair-dryer.

Some cats, rather like small boys, utterly detest the idea of bathing, and can make a terrible fuss when trundled into the bathroom. If you really cannot get your moggy dunked, settle for second best – a dry shampoo. Heat some bran in the oven and then work it well into the cat's coat. Brush the bran out thoroughly and repeat. Continue the sequence until the coat is respectable once more.

You may have a kitten that is either too slow-witted or too lazy to begin washing itself. It quickly cottons on if you smear a little anchovy paste or Gentleman's Relish onto its fur. For a Siamese it might be more proper to apply a soupçon of pâté de foie gras de Strasbourg.

Ears need cleaning once a week. Do not pour powders down them. Wipe them out with a 'baby bud' or twist of cotton wool moistened in olive oil.

But thousands die, without or this or that,
Die, and endow a college, or a cat.
Alexander Pope: *Moral Essays*, referring to
the Duchess of Richmond, who had left
annuities for the benefit of her cats

Veterans

Inevitably, time catches up with cats. Should your pet
survive beyond seventeen years, he is doing very well indeed. Very few reach one score, although the longevity
record at present stands as thirty-four years achieved by a
tabby queen from Devon – a tribute to the salutary virtues
of a daily helping of clotted cream, perhaps. Certainly cats
tend to last longer than dogs, where the majority do not
pass sixteen and the record is twenty-seven.

Old cats need special attention and understanding. After
years of faithful companionship it would be a churlish
owner who did not give a thought to coping with feline
geriatrics.

Venerable cats change physically. They frequently become rather thin. This may be accompanied by a change in
appetite with an increased or decreased demand for food.
They may become more thirsty. Certainly some of these are
the results of failing liver and kidneys, conditions which, in
the absence of other symptoms, are difficult for the vet to
deal with.

If your cat's appetite increases, give more food at each
meal or, better, more meals daily. High-quality protein
food (fish, meat, poultry) and a variety of vegetables and
fruit are essential for the pussy pensioner. Give him more
water or milk if he wants it; denying the increased thirst
would be dangerous.

Age may bring fussiness, and concentration on high-

quality protein may produce bowel sluggishness and constipation as happens in some old people. Although oily
fish like tinned pilchards help the free movement of the
bowel, the basic fault generally is that in providing rich and
tasty morsels to the old-timer, owners do not give enough
bulky roughage, the stuff that gives healthy exercise to the
intestines. A little paraffin oil (liquid paraffin) mixed with
the food can be used occasionally as a laxative (say two
teaspoonfuls once or twice weekly), but the regular daily
use of paraffin oil is bad, as it cuts down the absorption by
the cat of the vitamins A, D and E in his diet.

If Puss will not take fibre in his food in the form of All-
Bran or crumbled toasted wholemeal bread, the daily use of
a bulk-acting granular laxative is the answer. An ideal one
is Vi-Siblin, made from certain plant seed husks. Laxatives
of this type are usually well accepted by cats when mixed

with the meat or fish. Once swallowed, they absorb liquid, swell and make bulk that stimulates contraction of the lazy intestine-wall muscles.

In old age a special watch should be kept on the mouth. Regular servicing by the vet throughout life should have stopped the build-up of tartar. A fondness for soft snacks in Pussy's dotage may encourage rapid tartar formation with secondary gum damage, inflammation in the tooth sockets and loosening teeth. Catch these things early. Septic areas in the mouth and bad teeth can only contribute to kidney and liver run-down. General anaesthesia for major mouth surgery (multiple extractions etc) can be risky in old age, so do not neglect cat mouth hygiene in young and middle age. Deal with tartar when you first see it. Clean the old cat's teeth once or twice weekly with a soft toothbrush or cotton-wool dipped in salt and water.

There is a tendency for cats to lose personal pride when past their prime. With the days long past for courting the young queen next door or snappily promenading one's territory like a Parisian boulevardier, with the ingle nook or familiar old armchair meaning more than roof-top romance or High Noon confrontations with the battle-scarred tom from across the tracks, sartorial standards fall. Puss either forgets or cannot be bothered to groom himself. In long-haired cats watch out for cots building up in the coat. Groom daily with comb and brush.

Some old warriors lose control of their bowels or water-works on the odd occasion. It may be forgetfulness. It may be that nerve control of the various valves involved is weakening. If it becomes troublesome, let your vet check over the animal. Cystitis can be a cause of involuntary 'leaking' and should be treated. Lazy bowels may simply need more of the bulk content mentioned on page 35.

Deafness or failing eyesight usually arise gradually if at all, and the owner should be able to compensate intelligently for them. For example, remember that a deaf cat cannot hear if you are moving furniture, vacuuming the carpet or bringing a strange dog into the room – all potential dangers from the immediate vicinity of which a cat with good hearing will quickly remove himself. With a blind cat, keep his food dishes in the same place and protect him from open fires and similar dangers; try to avoid re-arranging familiar furniture.

Although there is no elixir of life available yet for man or his pets, there are some drugs which the veterinarian may prescribe that can counteract some of the symptoms of old age. One is sulphadiazine, which is claimed to combat senility, lack of lustre, greying of hair and general lack of interest and vitality where such signs are due solely to old age. Others are the range of anabolic hormones which encourage tissue building, oppose wastage of bodily protein, speed the healing processes and generally increase appetite, alertness and activity. The vet must decide whether your cat is suitable for treatment with any of these compounds.

DEATH

In ancient Egypt, folk would shave off their eyebrows as a token of deepest grief if a cat died naturally. If you are fortunate, Puss will die in his sleep when his time comes. Alternatively you, as a humane and responsible owner, may have to make the tough decision for him. If a cat is in pain that is not likely to be quickly relieved, if the condition is a hopeless one where the animal is literally dis-eased and obviously unhappy, or if it is an embarrassment to itself (paralyzed, continually fouling itself etc), then it is false sentimentality and irresponsible petmanship to deny the creature a dignified end.

Euthanasia is merciful and only an extension of deep general anaesthesia. Avoid humane society clinics where animals are euthanased by lay staff or where electrocution or chloroform boxes are used.

The vet will perform euthanasia by injecting an overdose of an anaesthetic (usually a barbiturate) either intravenously or into the chest. There is no more pain than that associated with any needle prick. Do not fret if Puss goes to sleep slowly and takes several minutes to stop breathing. The drugs are totally painless anaesthetics being used in over-dose. Rapid, painful poisons like cyanide and strychnine are never used.

It may be a touchy subject, but as a cat-lover you are interested in the welfare of our feline friends as a whole. If the vet suggests that a post-mortem examination may be of value, try to agree. Your old friend will feel nothing but may contribute something of great value to the continual advancement of pet health.

10

Breakdowns

The arts of medicine and surgery relating to the cat, be it a blue-blooded show specimen or an alley cat, are now highly sophisticated veterinary specialities. The problems that can afflict the species are being increasingly researched and much is known about both how similar and how different cats are compared to dogs or humans when unwell or in trouble.

An intricate machine needs a skilled mechanic. Do not tinker with your cat. My main aim in this section of the book will be to explain symptoms, what you should do about them and simple, useful first-aid with an emphasis on the 'first'. Seek veterinary help for all but the mildest and briefest conditions. I will also outline the basic principles behind the commoner diseases of cats, together with the ways in which the vet counter-attacks these afflictions.

But in all your pet's ailments, mild or serious, you will normally have to be prepared to do something, usually acting as nurse. There are some essential nursing techniques to be learned.

HANDLING A CAT FOR EXAMINATION

The five main methods are:

Method 1   Cradling in the arms if the animal is quiet and not in pain.
Method 2   Restraint holding all four legs.

Method 3   Holding by the 'scruff' and pressing down firmly onto a flat surface to restrict the scratching ability of the paws.

Method 4   The perspex cylinder method.

Method 5   Wrapping in a large strong cloth, sack or blanket.

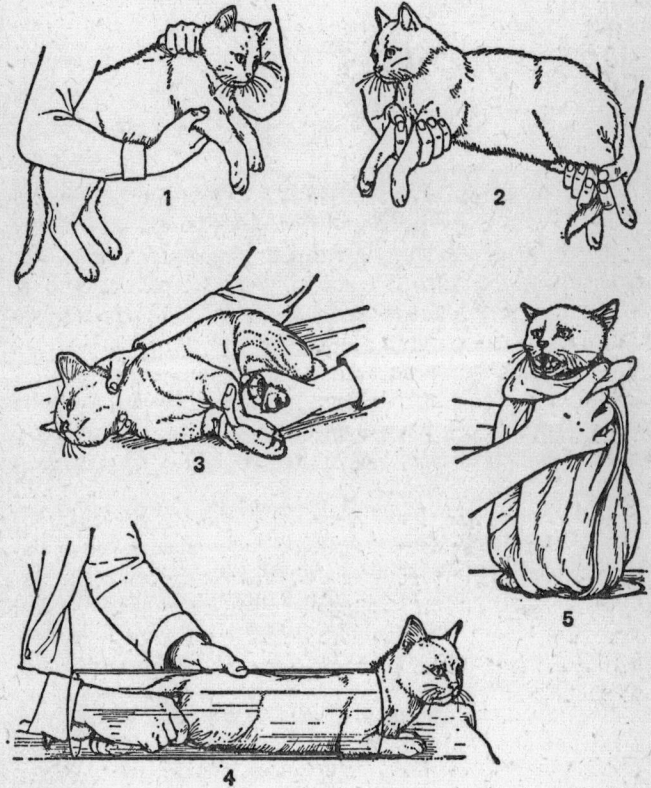

ADMINISTERING MEDICINE

Not easy, ever. Although the vet will try to select drug preparations as attractive as possible to cats, liquids and crushed tablets mixed with the food are usually detected quickly. Puss then marches off in high dudgeon, going without a meal rather than taking his medicine.

The key technique to master is holding the cat's head as shown, bending it back on the neck until the mouth automatically opens a fraction. Then keep the mouth open

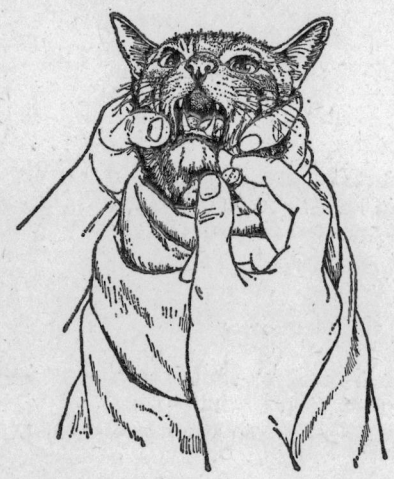

by pushing the lips on each side between the teeth with your index finger and thumb. If giving a tablet, drop it accurately onto the groove at the back of the tongue. Give a quick poke with the index finger of the other hand (or carefully with a pencil if you feel timid about your finger's safety), pushing the tablet over the back of the tongue. Close the mouth immediately.

With the same grip on the head, liquids can be dropped in slowly. Do not be impatient and flood your pet's mouth with fluid. The cat will only choke, panic and splutter furiously.

Injections
Done by the vet, this is normally the slickest, easiest means of giving cats drugs.

Pre-tranquillising

If your cat is as wild as a mountain lion but has to be taken to the vet's surgery for some reason, it is often possible to make things easier for all concerned by giving valium or some other sedative under the vet's instructions before leaving home.

TAKING TEMPERATURES

This is done by inserting a thermometer in the rectum. Cat books generally regard it as 'important'. Forget it. Most cats object to this undignified intrusion, become excited and the temperature climbs anyway. If you insist on going ahead, the normal temperature is 100·5–101·5°F.

GOING OUT OF TUNE

Like Alice I shall begin at the beginning and look at the mouth of the cat. After the mouth we shall together wander from head to tail through the various systems of the feline body.

The mouth

This sharp end of the animal should be inspected from time to time to see if all is in order. Once or twice weekly cleaning of the teeth with cotton wool or a soft toothbrush dipped in salt water will stop the build-up of troublesome tartar. I can hear you saying that no-one cleans their cat's teeth that often, but it would save untold problems for the older cat if you will spend a few moments every two or three days on this very easy job. The feeding of coarsely cut raw butcher's meat occasionally will also help.

If tartar, a brown, cement-like substance, accumulates to any extent, it does not produce holes in the teeth that need filling. Instead it damages the gum edge, lets bacteria in to infect the tooth socket and thus loosens teeth. There is always some gum inflammation (gingivitis) with tartar.

Commonest symptoms. Salivating (slavering), pawing at the mouth, exaggerated chewing motions, tentative chewing as if dealing with a hot potato.

What you can do. Open the mouth and look for a foreign body stuck between the teeth. A piece of bone often wedges between the teeth and against the roof of the mouth. Fishbone pieces sometimes lodge between two adjacent molars at the back of the mouth. You can probably flick a foreign body out with a teaspoon handle or similar instrument. If there is no foreign body, look for smooth red ulcerated areas on the tongue. These can be caused by licking an irritant substance but are more commonly caused by the virus of Ulcerative Glossitis, a member of the Feline Influenza group. Ulcers of this type are usually associated with profuse slavering, unwillingness to eat and some dullness. Get veterinary help, since a course of antibiotic injections may be needed to prevent secondary infection. The third alternative is loose, diseased teeth. Touch each tooth gently with your finger or a pencil. Look for wobbling of the tooth or some sign of pain from the cat. Do *not* give aspirin to relieve suspected toothache; *aspirin is poisonous to cats.*

Feline dentistry is easily tackled by the vet. He has the anaesthetics, de-scalers and drugs to attend to mouth problems. If many teeth have to be removed from an elderly cat, do not worry. Food such as minced cooked liver, fish and cereals with milk are easily taken even by totally toothless moggies. No teeth at all is better than having septic gums and rotten teeth that create misery and can poison the whole system.

The eyes

Commonest symptoms. Sore, runny or mattery eyes. A blue or white film over the eye. The protrusion of a white skin (the haw, third eyelid or nictitating membrane) over some or most of one or both eyes from the inner corner.

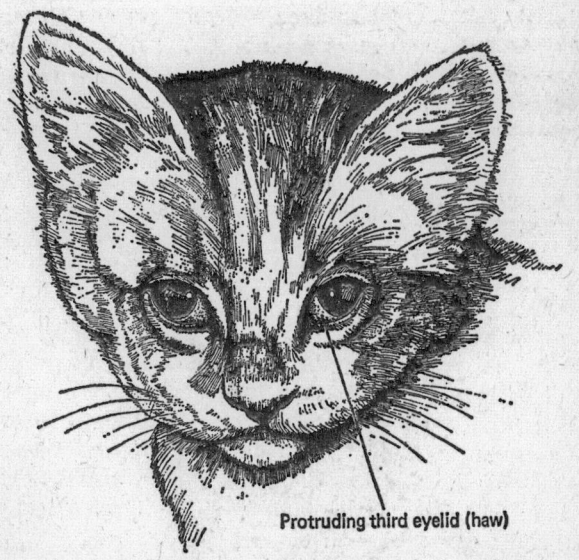

Protruding third eyelid (haw)

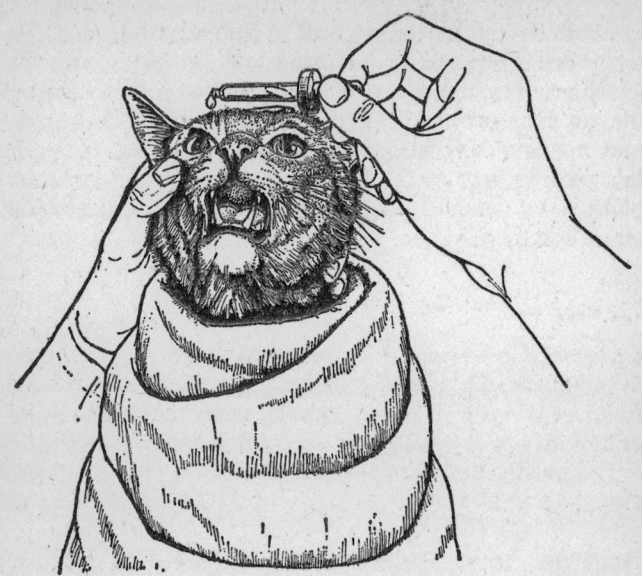

What you can do. If the eye is obviously sore and inflamed, if the eyeball has a blue or white area on it, or if the lids are swollen, then infection, wounding or foreign bodies such as grass awns may be involved. If the cat is not very concerned you can drop Brolene liquid (available from the chemists) into the affected eye – one drop three times daily. For more troublesome or persistent cases, see the vet.

The partial covering of the eye by the third eyelid is a common and curious phenomenon. It often happens in otherwise apparently healthy cats. It can be as a result of weight loss, when the eye sinks back as the fat padding within the eye socket is reduced. It may be an early symptom of Feline Influenza. The cat is *not* going blind. Keep a careful watch on the creature. Should other symptoms develop, see the vet. If it persists for long without other signs, try boosting the food intake and give fifty micrograms of vitamin B_{12} daily in the food or as a tablet.

The veterinarian has a number of ways of dealing with the varieties of eye disease. He can use local anaesthetic drops to numb the eye for the removal of irritant objects and can apply drugs not just by ointment and drops but also by injection under the conjunctiva, the pink membrane round the eye. He can examine deep into the eye with his ophthalmoscope and identify infecting bacteria by taking swabs of the cat's tears. Nowadays the vet can deal with squint, blocked tear ducts, cataractous lenses and many other conditions by surgery.

The nose

Commonest symptoms. Running, mattery nostrils. Snuffling. Sneezing. The appearance of symptoms like those of the common cold in humans generally means an outbreak of Feline Influenza (see pages 74–5). After recovery from the latter disease, many cats remain snuffly and catarrhal for months or years.

What you can do. Bathe the delicate nose tip with warm water. Soften and remove caked mucus. Anoint a little vaseline into the nose. Feline Influenza needs veterinary attention.

The ears

Commonest symptoms. Shaking the head, scratching the ear. Tilting of the head to one side, sometimes associated with loss of balance and a staggering gait. Sudden 'ballooning' of an ear flap. Tiny white 'insects' moving slowly around inside the ear. A bad-smelling, chocolate-coloured or purulent discharge.

What you can do. If ear trouble flares up suddenly, pour in liberal quantities of paraffin oil (liquid paraffin) warmed to body heat. Do it in the garage; Puss will flick excess oil all over your chintz curtains if you do it in the lounge.

If the cat is simply an ear-flicker and the ears seem dry but contain the 'insects' referred to above (actually otodectic mange mites), get some ear mange drops from the pet-shop.

Any discharge constitutes canker and may need antibiotic treatment by the vet. Head-tilting and loss of balance may indicate Otitis Media (middle ear disease). This is inflammation behind the ear-drum in the middle ear. Infection usually enters this area via a channel (the Eustachian tube) that runs from the throat, so it often follows throat and respiratory infections. It needs immediate veterinary treatment, since the modern drugs used by the vet can reach the inflammation in the middle ear and in almost all cases prevent permanent damage to the balancing organs and the spread of the infection to the brain. Middle ear disease is quite common in lion cubs.

The sudden ballooning of the ear flap of a cat is due to bleeding within the flap. It is a haematoma, really just a big blood blister, usually as a result of the cat scratching its own ear vigorously but sometimes caused by a blow or bite from another animal. It annoys the cat because it feels strangely heavy but is not painful like an abscess unless secondarily infected, which is uncommon. The cat shakes its head trying to dislodge the weight. The condition is identical to that seen in human boxers who are repeatedly cuffed round the ears. Left untreated, the blood inside the haematoma clots and shrinks into a gnarled scar, crumpling the ear into a 'cauliflower'.

The vet can avoid Puss taking on the appearance of a punchy prize-fighter by giving a general anaesthetic, draining off the blood, usually through an incision, and then stitching the ear in a special way that may involve attaching steel buttons for a week or so. It is not a serious condition and the success rate following surgery is very high. Nevertheless, the cause of the original scratching (mites, canker or whatever) must be treated simultaneously to avoid a recurrence.

The chest

Commonest symptoms. Coughing, gasping, laboured breathing. Cats can suffer from bronchitis, pneumonia, pleurisy and other chest conditions. Coughing and sneezing – all the miserable signs of a head cold – may be signs of Feline Influenza (cat 'flu). This disease is also caused by a virus. It may be mild or severe and sometimes ends fatally. In such cases the damage may be done by secondary bacterial infections of the lung. It is not a cold, wet weather disease particularly: many major outbreaks occur in summer and it is often found in epidemic form in catteries during the hot holiday months. Laboured breathing without 'cold' symptoms may be a sign of pleurisy or of heart disease in older cats.

What you can do. Protect your cat against Feline Influenza by ensuring that he is vaccinated and boosted regularly. Incidentally, there is no connection between human and cat forms of 'flu. Keep a cat with chest trouble warm and dry. Do not let him exert himself. Give him nutritious food, finely minced or liquid, if he will accept it. There is no harm in the odd drop of brandy or whisky spooned in. Keep the nostrils unblocked as far as possible by sponging the

nose and greasing it with a little vaseline. In simple cases where the cat continues to eat and his breathing is not too distressed, a quarter of a teaspoonful of Benylin syrup obtainable from your chemist may be given every two or three hours as a cough mixture.

More serious cases will be treated by the vet using anti-biotics, drugs to loosen mucus in the lungs and, where the heart is involved, special cardiac medicines. Where fluid accumulates in the chest in pleurisy cases, the vet may tap this off under sedation. Very many cats with dicky hearts can live happy, long lives once their problem has been diagnosed and maintenance treatment prescribed.

The stomach and intestines

Commonest symptoms. Vomiting, diarrhoea, constipation, blood in the droppings. There are numerous causes for any of these symptoms and sometimes more than one symptom will be observed at the same time. I shall deal only with commonest symptoms, and not attempt to describe all the diseases which can involve the abdominal organs.

Vomiting may be simple and transient, due to a mild infection (gastritis) of the stomach or the presence of a fur-ball. If severe, persistent or accompanied by other major signs, however, it can indicate the presence of serious conditions such as Feline Infectious Enteritis, tumours or obstruction of the intestine.

Diarrhoea may be simple, the result of too much liver or a mild bowel infection. It may be more serious and profuse, as in some cases of Feline Infectious Enteritis.

Constipation may be a result of age and faulty diet or an indicator of obstruction.

Blood in the stools may be merely from the scratching of the intestinal lining by gobbled bone splinters, or the effect of an acute food-poisoning attack.

What you can do. Use your common sense. If any of these symptoms persists for more than a few hours or is accom-panied by profound malaise and weakness on the part of the cat, you need skilled help. In simple cases or until the vet arrives, remember that water and salt loss through vomiting or diarrhoea is the killing factor. You can do something to combat this. Spoon frequent small quantities of glucose and water, seasoned to your taste with table salt, into the cat. Where vomiting is the prime symptom, give no solid food but concentrate on the liquid replacement. Persevere if vomiting continues. Do *not* use milk or brandy. Half a teaspoonful of Milk of Magnesia or baby gripe water can be given.

Where diarrhoea is the main sign, again concentrate on fluid administration. Gently introducing a third of a cupful of strong sweetened coffee at body temperature via the rectum through a human enema syringe is safe and sensible; do it slowly. A teaspoonful of Kaopectate mixture can be given by mouth. Do *not* try human kaolin and morphine diarrhoea mixtures.

In the early stages of constipation try spooning two or three teaspoonsful of paraffin oil (liquid paraffin) into the cat. The tiny, ready-to-use Micralax enemas available at the chemist are excellent and very effective. Use a half to one tube as directed for humans on the accompanying instructions. Where constipation is a chronic problem, add bulk to the diet and use Vi-Siblin or Iso-Gel granules sprinkled on the food to make artificial bulk.

Severe or persistent cases need veterinary attention. The vet can examine the alimentary tract with his fingers, by X-ray, possibly by barium meals, by stethoscope, by gastroscope and sometimes by exploratory operation.

Feline Infectious Enteritis, one of the major virus diseases of cats, is not purely a complaint affecting the intestines; it attacks the liver and white cells of the blood also. It can run a very short and fatal course in a matter of hours and the symptoms are variable. Diarrhoea is not always present. Although the vet cannot kill the virus, he may use antibiotics such as chloroamphenicol against secondary bacterial attack. He will certainly be concerned to protect the cat from dehydrating through fluid loss, and this may mean transfusions of saline under the skin. The best cure for Feline Infectious Enteritis, a terrible scourge, is prevention. Have your cat vaccinated and boosted regularly.

Urinary system

Commonest symptoms. Difficulty passing urine, blood in urine. Loss of weight. Thirst. Cats on mainly dry-food diets, cats taking insufficient water and tom cats castrated very early are more prone to develop 'gravel' in the urine. This deposit of salt crystals in the bladder can eventually block up the urethra (water pipe) of male animals. The cat strains to pass urine and owners may mistake the position adopted for one of constipation. When the bladder is over-full and tight as a drum the cat is in considerable pain, will resent being handled and may actually turn to look at its hind quarters and spit angrily. Do *not* try squeezing the cat's swollen bladder yourself. It is very easily ruptured.

Blood in the urine generally indicates bladder infection (cystitis). This complaint is commoner in females. It too requires veterinary treatment.

Loss of weight and thirst, particularly in old cats, can be due to kidney disease although other diseases including diabetes can exhibit these signs.

What you can do. As a preventive measure, make sure your cat always has plenty of fresh water available and a good proportion of moist food. Do not have a tom castrated too early.

The vet can deal with urinary problems using special urine-active antiseptics and antibiotics. He can catheterise a cat's bladder painlessly to free blockages and take urine samples for analysis. The kidneys can be X-rayed by contrast radiography and, if necessary, the bladder and urethra can be operated upon quite safely.

Genitalia

Commonest symptoms. Concerning ourself solely with the female, the major symptom is a purulent discharge of some colour (white, pink, yellow, chocolate) from the vagina. Obviously in cats known to be pregnant this calls for immediate veterinary attention. In non-pregnant queens it can be a sign of womb infection (usually following kittening) or the onset of the hormonal disease, pyometra. This is commonest in queens which have never had kittens or maybe just one litter. It looks like a septic infection and can make the animal very ill through absorption of the nasty fluid that distends the womb, although in many cases the pus is sterile. It is not an infectious disease although secondary bacterial invasions are a danger.

What you can do. If you are not planning on breeding, have a female speyed when young. If discharges are seen, clean the vulval area with warm water and weak antiseptic and take the little lady along to the vet.

The vet may use hormone treatment together with drugs

such as quinine to reduce the amount of fluid in the womb and antibiotics to tackle any opportunist bugs. His main weapon is normally surgical: hysterectomy, the removal of the diseased womb through a side or mid-line incision under general anaesthetic. If Puss is in a weak and toxic state because of the diseased womb, he may delay operating for some time in order to try to strengthen her with vitamins, anti-toxic drugs and antibiotics.

The skin

There are many kinds of skin disease in cats. Diagnosis needs examination and often sample-analysis by the vet.

Commonest symptoms. Thin or bald patches in the fur, scratching, wet or dry sores. Irritating mange caused by an invisible mite can cause dry, motheaten-looking areas

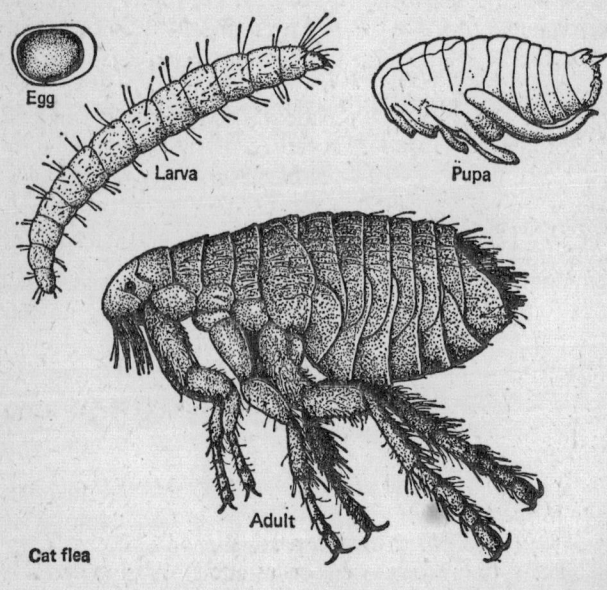

Egg

Larva

Pupa

Adult

Cat flea

round the head and ears. Itchy thinning of the hair over the trunk with points of oozing red scabs is one of the commonest skin diseases. Often named 'Fish Eczema', this complaint has nothing to do with eating fish but is glandular in origin. Fleas and less commonly lice and ticks can cause damage to the coat. The presence of just one single flea on a cat – terribly hard to track down – may set up widespread itchy skin irritation as an allergic reaction to the flea's saliva injected when the little devil sucks. In late summer, orange specks in the fur of the head and ears or between the toes reveal the presence of harvest mites.

What you can do. If you see or suspect the presence of any of the skin parasites – fleas, lice, ticks, mites – obtain one of the anti-parasitic aerosols or powders for cats from the pet-shop or chemist. *Never* use DDT on cats. Gamma BHC is suitable, as are pybuthrin preparations. Remember that parasites are most numerous in hot weather.

If necessary, have the cause of your pet's tatty upholstery investigated by the vet. He will prescribe different drugs for the various types of disease. Ringworm, a very subtle thing in cats compared to the form it takes in man or cattle, may need ultra-violet light examination or fungus culture from a hair specimen for diagnosis, but can now be treated by drugs given orally. Mange can be attacked from outside or inside – by baths, creams or aerosols or by tablets which work via the bloodstream. 'Fish Eczema' is treated by hormone tablets.

WORMS

There are two main kinds of worm which infest cats: roundworms and tapeworms.

Roundworms
These can cause bowel upsets, particularly in kittens. They can spread to humans and occasionally damage babies severely.

Rid your cat of roundworms by giving one of the modern worming drugs (piperazine, mebendazole, dichlorvos etc) at regular three-month intervals throughout his life.

Tapeworms

These worms do not often cause the cat much trouble but they can occasionally spread to humans. They have a life-cycle passing through fleas.

Keep your cat free of fleas (see page 81). If you see tapeworm segments (they look like grains of boiled rice) in the stools or stuck to the hair round the anus, give the cat a dose of one of the modern tapeworm drugs such as bunamidine or niclosamide. The very safe worming drug, mebendazole, eradicates both roundworms and tapeworms in the cat, so with regular use of this drug you can kill two birds with one stone very easily.

BITES AND OTHER WOUNDS

The story is told of two cats which fought so ferociously that when the battle was over only the tail of each was left. It is in fact an allegory for the feud between the two towns of Kilkenny and Irishtown in Ireland, who fought so persistently over boundaries and rights up to the end of the seventeenth century that they both ended up bankrupt. So 'to fight like the Kilkenny Cats' is to end up with a pyrrhic victory on both sides.

Kilkenny or not, cats do fight and often get bitten, particularly un-neutered toms who frequent low company. Bites tend to go septic and can prove troublesome. They may produce abscesses which on the torso tend to be soft, low swellings covering a wide area. Hidden by the fur, they may show no signs except pain when the cat is handled. They are not always easy to detect by probing with the fingers. On the limbs or tail, where the bone lies close to the surface, it is common for bacteria to reach the surface of the bone when an attacker's canine teeth pierce the skin. Septic wounds of the feet can show themselves as dramatically enlarged 'club paws', and bites to the tail can threaten

the extremity with the onset of gangrene.

As soon as you detect a bite wound, clip the hair around it down to the skin with scissors. Apply a strong solution of Epsom salts (magnesium sulphate crystals) in warm water to the wound as frequently as possible. Antiseptic ointments are of little value as the bacteria have been 'injected' by the biter's teeth. A single long-acting shot of penicillin from the vet is a prudent measure.

Where the animal is found to have an abscess, swollen limb or septic tail already, professional treatment is essential.

Other types of wound where the skin is torn should be bathed in weak antiseptic and warm water, dried and sprinkled with sulpha powder. Veterinary treatment will be needed for wounds that are of a size to need stitching. Small wounds, if contaminated with soil etc, and particularly old or puncture wounds, will benefit greatly from antibiotic therapy.

Humans bitten or scratched by cats should regard their

wounds as potentially dangerous. There is the possibility of infection with the germs of 'cat scratch fever' or with the bacterium often found in cats' mouths, *Pasteurella septica.*

ACCIDENTS

Cats do occasionally appear to have nine lives. Their bodies are so elastic and wiry that they often survive being run over by a car tyre without suffering fractures or serious damage. Nevertheless they do get their share of accidents. Hit by cars, airgun pellets, stones, falling masonry or drunkards' boots, trapped in doors, falling from great heights or savaged by dogs, Puss sometimes seems to need every life he can lay claim to. These serious crises produce skeleton and soft-tissue damage which the vet will have to sort out in the operating room. Your job is to render useful first-aid emergency treatment until the animal can be taken to the vet or vice versa.

First, get the patient into a quiet, warm place indoors. Slip a sheet underneath him and carry him as in a hammock or with one hand by the scruff of the neck. Do not waste time or stand on ceremony. Shock is your principal adversary. Lay him comfortably on a warm blanket. Place a hot (not scalding) water bottle next to him.

Do not give alcoholic stimulants. Do not give aspirin. You may try to spoon in a few teaspoonsful of warm sweet tea.

If something is bleeding badly, slap a thick pad of cotton wool, lint or a folded handkerchief on the place and press firmly – if necessary until the vet arrives.

Do not try splinting fractured limbs. Leave them alone.

In life-or-death cases of drowning or choking where you cannot easily remove whatever is causing the obstruction you must literally swing a cat. Pick him up by his two hind legs and whirl him round and round. The idea is that centrifugal force will drive blockages from the airways. Do not be namby-pamby about this; swing him hard. It is difficult to dislocate a cat's legs, and better dislocated than dead. After this, if necessary, try artificial respiration. Make sure the tongue is not lying back in the mouth. Use either manual squeezing of the chest (*not too hard* – I have seen lungs and hearts severely injured by over-vigorous life-savers) or 'mouth to mouth' respiration, taking the whole of the cat's muzzle in your mouth.

Remember that it saves time to be doing all this (except perhaps the cat-swinging) in a car on the way to the vet's surgery, rather than waiting for the vet to come to you.

Much more could be written about this most fascinating of animals, but Lenin, my own faithful Puss, is wearing his lean and hungry look. First let me slice his cooked mackerel and then I shall say, like Swinburne in *To a Cat*,

> 'Stately, kindly, lordly friend,
>   Condescend
> Here to sit by me.'

Index

Also available in this series

THE DOG

David Taylor is a well-known veterinary surgeon and the author of three books about his work as a wildlife vet: *Zoovet, Doctor in the Zoo* and *Going Wild*. He has also been a regular guest on BBC television's *Animal Magic* where he has advised on less exotic animals – the family pet. *The Dog*, one of a series of practical books by David Taylor, gives specialist, helpful and humorous advice on living with and caring for your dog. Everything the dog lover needs to know is presented in this book with the aid of diagrams and some light-hearted cartoons.

In preparation

THE PONY
THE SMALL PET
THE CAGE BIRD
THE EXOTIC PET